CONTENTS

HIGH IN THE SKY

Steve Parker

WALKER BOOKS
AND SUBSIDIARIES
LONDON · BOSTON · SYDNEY

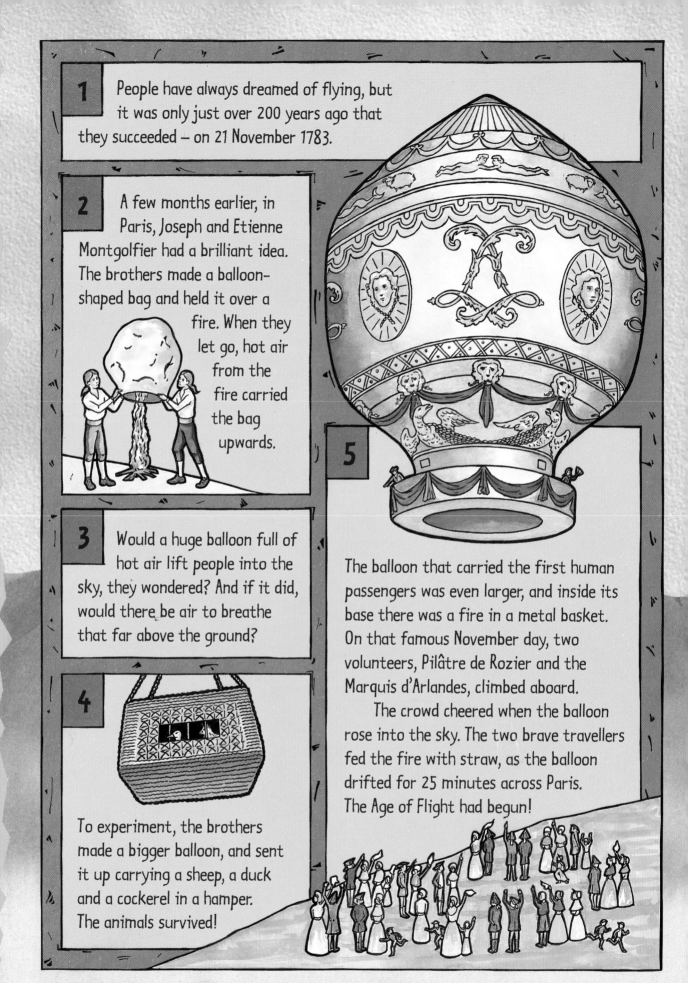

1 People have always dreamed of flying, but it was only just over 200 years ago that they succeeded – on 21 November 1783.

2 A few months earlier, in Paris, Joseph and Etienne Montgolfier had a brilliant idea. The brothers made a balloon-shaped bag and held it over a fire. When they let go, hot air from the fire carried the bag upwards.

3 Would a huge balloon full of hot air lift people into the sky, they wondered? And if it did, would there be air to breathe that far above the ground?

4 To experiment, the brothers made a bigger balloon, and sent it up carrying a sheep, a duck and a cockerel in a hamper. The animals survived!

5 The balloon that carried the first human passengers was even larger, and inside its base there was a fire in a metal basket. On that famous November day, two volunteers, Pilâtre de Rozier and the Marquis d'Arlandes, climbed aboard.

The crowd cheered when the balloon rose into the sky. The two brave travellers fed the fire with straw, as the balloon drifted for 25 minutes across Paris. The Age of Flight had begun!

2 HOT-AIR BALLOONS

UP, UP AND AWAY

1 Can you imagine blowing up a balloon that's taller than a house? Hot-air balloons are huge — the balloon part is called the canopy, and it can be 25 metres high!

2 If you opened out the canopy and laid it flat, it would cover four tennis courts. It's made of long panels of rip-proof nylon, stitched together with 5 kilometres of thread.

3 The pilot and passengers ride inside a wicker basket. It's like a big shopping basket, but much thicker and sturdier.

HOT-AIR BALLOONS 3

4 Wicker is very strong, but also very light. All parts of the balloon have to be as light as possible, because the only thing keeping the balloon up in the sky is...

5 ...hot air! The special thing about hot air is that it floats upwards. You've seen this happening if you've ever watched smoke rising above a bonfire.

6 Hot-air balloons have burners at the mouth of their canopy, where gas is burned to heat the air. The hot air rushes into the canopy and pushes it upwards, lifting the basket.

7 The gas fuel comes from bottles inside the basket. A dial shows how full the bottles are, so the pilot can land safely before the fuel runs out.

4 HOT-AIR BALLOONS

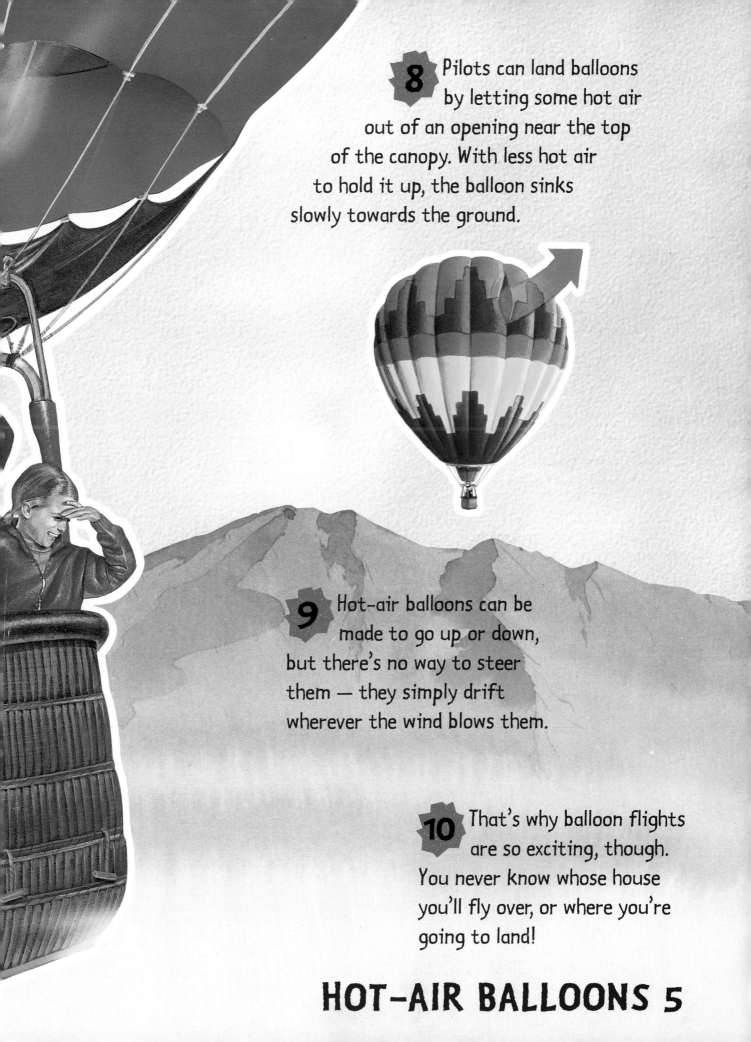

8 Pilots can land balloons by letting some hot air out of an opening near the top of the canopy. With less hot air to hold it up, the balloon sinks slowly towards the ground.

9 Hot-air balloons can be made to go up or down, but there's no way to steer them — they simply drift wherever the wind blows them.

10 That's why balloon flights are so exciting, though. You never know whose house you'll fly over, or where you're going to land!

HOT-AIR BALLOONS 5

SHIPS IN THE SKY

1 Is it a balloon? Is it a plane? No, it's a bit of both — an airship!

2 Airships float like balloons, but they don't use hot air. The balloon part is called the envelope, and it's filled with a very light gas called helium.

3 Balloons drift with the wind, but airships don't. Like planes, they have engines to power them along.

1 Seventy years ago, there were no big passenger planes flying around the world. If you had to travel a long way, you went by train, or ocean liner — or by airship.

2 Envelope

Boeing 747

Passenger area inside envelope

Pilot's gondola

These old airships were truly gigantic — some were over three times longer than today's jumbo jets. The passenger area was actually inside the envelope, but sealed off from the gas.

4 This airship's engines are on either side of the back of the gondola. This is the cabin under the envelope, and it's where the passengers and pilot ride.

5 Although airships have engines, they can't fly all that fast. So they're mainly used for things like sightseeing, when people want to travel slowly and quietly.

AUKO

3 The passenger area was like a hotel. You could lounge about listening to a piano player, eat a meal in the dining room, or snooze in your own bedroom.

Bedrooms

Dining room

Lounge

4 But in those days, airships were filled with hydrogen. And unlike helium, this gas catches fire easily. By the late 1930s, several airships had blown up, killing hundreds of people. No one would risk flying in them, and the age of giant airships came to an end.

AIRSHIPS 7

1 Flying a stunt plane is like riding the world's best roller-coaster, but you're in charge!

Joystick →

Rudder pedals →

2 Press one of the pedals. The rudder flap on the tail fin moves, turning the plane sideways. Niaawoow, you're swinging round.

3 Push the joystick to one side and hold it there. Aileron flaps on the main wings move and — oooooohh, you're rolling right over.

4 Now pull the joystick towards you. Elevator flaps on the tail wings tilt up, pushing the plane's tail down and its nose up. Wheeeeeee, you're zooming upwards.

5 Keep the joystick pulled back. You're looping up and right over — aaaaargh, where's the sick bag!

1 Why is this plane upside down? It's a stunt plane for doing special displays, twisting and looping around the sky. In a second, it'll turn the right way up again!

2 It's also a biplane, which means it has two pairs of wings. (Most planes are monoplanes, with just one pair.)

3 All planes have wings. They couldn't fly without them, because it's the wings that keep a plane up in the air.

8 WINGED FLIGHT

WONDER WINGS

5 This difference in air speeds creates a force called lift, which sucks the wings, and the plane, up into the sky.

4 Plane wings do this because they're a special shape — curved on top and flat underneath — which makes air flow faster above them than below.

6 And it isn't hard to work out that with two pairs of wings, biplanes have around twice as much lift!

ROCKETING ALONG

1 Back in 1947, this plane was the fastest thing on wings. It was called the Bell X-1, and it had the most powerful kind of engine in the world — a rocket.

2 The Bell X-1 was designed for just one job. It was to be the first plane to go supersonic — that means to travel faster than sound...

...and sound travels at over 1,100 kilometres an hour!

1 Air flowing over wings will lift a plane upwards. But it will only do this if the plane is moving forwards. This is what engines are for — to produce a strong forwards force called thrust.

2 The faster the plane, the more powerful the engine it needs. Heavy planes need more powerful engines, too — and usually more than one.

Engines

10 ENGINES

3 The tiny plane only had room inside for the pilot's cockpit and the rocket engine behind it.

4 The pilot's name was Chuck Yeager, and on 14 October 1947 he became the world's first supersonic human.

5 By 1953, jet engines were also powerful enough to take planes to supersonic speeds. Nowadays, many jet fighters fly at over twice the speed of sound. But only one jet airliner does — Concorde.

3 Many planes now have jet engines, and the most common kind has a big fan at the front. As the fan spins, it sucks air into the engine where it's burned with jet fuel. This creates a blast of hot gas, which roars out of the back of the engine and pushes the plane forwards.

Hot gas out

Cold air in

4 Rocket engines give the most thrust. They're similar to jet engines, but they burn fuel with other chemicals instead of air. Very few planes have them, though, because they're expensive, noisy, and use lots of fuel.

LOOK, NO ENGINE!

1 All planes have wings, but they don't all have engines. How do they fly without them? Well, one way is to use human power instead of engine power.

Gossamer Albatross

2 In 1979, American cyclist Bryan Allen puffed, panted and pedalled this strange-looking plane across the Channel, from England to France.

3 The plane's name is Gossamer Albatross, and it's really a flying bicycle.

4 The pilot pedals like mad to turn a bike chain. The chain turns the propeller at the back, and the spinning propeller pushes the plane along.

12 PEDAL POWER

5 Allen's Channel crossing was the world's first long-distance human-powered flight.

It wasn't fast, though — the 36-kilometre trip took 2 hours and 49 minutes.

6 But pedal power makes Albatross fly only because the plane is so light. The whole thing weighs less than the pilot!

1 Gliders are planes without any engine at all. They can't take off by themselves, so they're towed up by a propeller plane. Once the glider is airborne, it lets the tow line go.

2 Gliders have amazingly long wings, which give lots of lift. But without an engine, a glider can't reach the speed needed to get enough lift to stay up in the sky. It will slowly sink towards the ground, unless...

3 ...the pilot finds a gust of wind to carry the glider upwards, or catches a ride on some rising hot air — a thermal.

4 With plenty of wind and thermals, a skilful pilot can swoop and soar across the sky all day — just like the birds!

GOING TO WORK

1 A plane with a broken nose? No, the front of this aircraft swings upwards on massive hinges. It's a huge door into the plane's main body, the fuselage.

3 Cargo planes carry all sorts of loads around the world — everything from airmail to flowers, and racehorses to bulldozers.

2 This is an An-124, and it has almost twice as much room in its fuselage as a jumbo jet does. It doesn't have any seats, though, as it doesn't have any passengers — its job is carrying cargo.

14 CARGO PLANES

1 A fire has broken out in the middle of a forest, far from the nearest town. It would take a fire engine hours to reach the scene — but a fire plane can be there within minutes.

4 But when there's a disaster, such as an earthquake or a flood, cargo planes can rush in medicines and other emergency aid.

2 As the CL-415 Firebird swoops low over the flames, doors open under its fuselage. Out pours enough water to fill 100 bathtubs.

Doors

3 The Firebird needs more water, so it zooms off to a nearby lake. As the plane skims the lake surface, water is forced through the fuselage doors into special storage tanks.

5 One single An-124 can fly in as much as four truck-loads of supplies to a disaster area, and carry away 500 people to safety.

4 Within minutes the Firebird is back over the forest, water-bombing the flames again. After a few more trips, the fire will be out — and the danger to the forest plants and animals will be over.

1 Emergency! The tide is coming in, and two children are trapped on a rock. Luckily, someone has spotted the danger and phoned for help — here comes a rescue helicopter now.

2 The rescue crew is ready at the open side door. One of them is wearing a safety harness fixed to a strong metal cable. While the helicopter hovers overhead, she's lowered towards the children.

3 The rescuer puts a safety strap around one child, then they're both pulled up into the helicopter.

4 The rescuer is lowered again and the second child is plucked to safety — just in time, as waves crash over the rock. Now it's back to base, to get warm and dry.

1 Helicopters are often called choppers, because they make such a loud chopping sound. The noise comes from the long blades on top of the helicopter slicing through the air.

2 The blades are called rotors, and each one is really a whirling wing — longer and narrower than a plane wing, but still curved on top and flat underneath.

16 HELICOPTERS

GOING CHOPPING

4 If it only had rotors on top, the whole helicopter would spin round. The tail rotors stop this, by turning in another direction.

5 Most planes only fly forwards, and need runways for taking off and landing. But helicopters can go straight up or down, sideways, backwards, and even hover in one place.

6 Because they can go where normal aircraft can't, helicopters are used for special jobs — such as rescuing people or chasing criminals.

3 As the rotors whizz through the air, they create the upwards force called lift — just as plane wings do.

HIDE AND SEEK

1 This F-117 Nighthawk fighter plane is on a spying mission. Its weird shape makes it invisible to the enemy — but how?

2 Most planes can be "seen" from the ground by radar, even at night. They show up as blips of light on special screens. But the Nighthawk doesn't!

1 How do pilots see where they're going in the middle of the night, or when flying through thick cloud?

2 They use radar to "see" for them. The plane's radar equipment sends out invisible radio signals...

3 Its strange shape and special black paint scatter radar signals, stopping radar equipment from working properly.

4 So although the enemy may be watching their radar screens, they won't see any blips.

6 But it was designed to be stealthy, not speedy. And its disguise is so good that it can fly in, spy and escape — without anyone knowing it was there!

5 The Nighthawk flies at only 1,000 kilometres per hour — about as fast as a jet airliner.

...and these bounce back like echoes — off other aircraft, thick clouds, or anything else that's in the way!

3 A computer works out how far away objects are by timing how long the signals take to bounce back. Then it shows the objects as pictures or blips of light on the pilot's radar screen.

25
20
15
10
5
SCREEN

1 The world's very first air passenger was called Charlie Furnace. He worked with the Wright brothers, who built and flew the first powered aircraft in 1903. Orville Wright took a terrified Charlie up for a ride in 1908.

2 The first passenger planes flew in the 1920s. They were old propeller-driven bombers from World War I, and were so cold and uncomfortable that passengers were given hot-water bottles to cuddle.

3 By the 1930s, passenger planes had heaters, padded chairs, and even reading lights. But their engines weren't powerful enough to fly above clouds and stormy weather, so flights could be very bumpy.

4 By the 1950s, planes had jet engines and were able to fly much faster and higher. This made journeys much quicker — and smoother, so fewer people got airsick!

5 Modern jet airliners fly 10 kilometres or more above the ground, and cruise along at about 1,000 kilometres per hour — six times faster than the planes of the 1920s.

20 AIRLINERS

RIDE IN THE SKY

1 This Boeing 777 landed 20 minutes ago. Already, all 370 passengers have gone — through the box-shaped walkway into the airport building. Even so, the plane is far from empty and quiet.

2 It's turnaround time. The plane must be checked, cleaned, fuelled, reloaded and ready to take off with new passengers, in less than an hour.

AIRLINERS 21

3 The ground crew is connecting pipes so the plane can be refuelled.

4 The pipes join an underground storage tank to the plane's main fuel tanks, in the wings.

5 It only takes 15 minutes to pump in enough fuel to fill 1,000 family cars. The pink liquid isn't car fuel, though. It's jet fuel, kerosene.

6 Meanwhile, the passenger cabin is being cleaned. When you flush a plane's toilet, the waste doesn't spray out into the air. It goes into a tank. During turnaround, this is emptied by a waste-disposal truck.

7 Baggage handlers are now loading the next flight's luggage into the holds, beneath the cabin floor.

8 Catering trucks are delivering food and drinks to the plane's kitchens, the galleys.

9 The new passengers will be on board soon, and the plane will be taxiing out to the main runway for take-off. Here we go again!

AIRLINERS 23

INDEX

Main illustrations by Andy Burton (18-19, 21-23); Roger Goode (cover, 8-9, 10-11, 22-23 cutaway); Mike Lister (3, 5); Darren Pattenden (4-5); Richard Morris (14-15); Tim Taylor (6-7, 15 inset); Darrell Warner (12-13, 16-17); inset and picture-strip illustrations by Ian Thompson.

With thanks to Beehive Illustration, Folio, and Helicopter Graphix.

Designed by Jonathan Hair and Matthew Lilly; edited by Jackie Gaff and Paul Harrison.

First published 1997 by Walker Books Ltd, 87 Vauxhall Walk, London SE11 5HJ

2 4 6 8 10 9 7 5 3 1

Text © 1997 Steve Parker
Illustrations © 1997 Walker Books Ltd

This book has been typeset in Kosmik.

Printed in Italy

British Library Cataloguing in Publication Data
A catalogue record for this book is available from the British Library.

ISBN 0-7445-2879-8

QUIZ ANSWERS

Page 2 — FALSE
A Portuguese priest, Father Gusmao, made a model hot-air balloon and flew it in 1709.

Page 6 — FALSE
The helium gas is in big bags called cells. These are inside the airship's envelope, and protected by it.

Page 9 — TRUE
They're called triplanes. Some early planes had up to nine pairs of wings!

Page 10 — FALSE
Rocket planes first flew in the 1930s.

Page 12 — TRUE
The space shuttle flies into space using rockets, but glides back down to Earth.

Page 14 — FALSE
Its 69-m-long fuselage makes the An-124 the second biggest. A stretched version, the An-225, has a 77-m-long fuselage and is the world's largest plane.

Page 17 — TRUE
But not all helicopters can loop right the way round and over, only the latest designs such as the Lynx.

Page 18 — FALSE
Radar was invented in 1935 and first used in planes in the 1940s.

Page 20 — TRUE
The captain or the co-pilot usually takes the controls for take-off and landing, but the autopilot (a computer) often flies the plane at other times.